Monster Trucks

Tom Morr and Ken Brubaker

MBI

This edition published in 2004 by MBI, an imprint of
MBI Publishing Company, Galtier Plaza, Suite 200,
380 Jackson Street, St. Paul, MN 55101-3885 USA

First published in 2003 by MBI Publishing Company.

MBI titles are also available at discounts in bulk quantity for
industrial or sales-promotional use. For details write to
Special Sales Manager at Motorbooks International
Wholesalers & Distributors, Galtier Plaza, Suite 200,
380 Jackson Street, St. Paul, MN 55101-3885 USA.

ISBN 0-7603-2028-4

On the front cover: John Hartsock launches Sudden Impact
with authority.

On the frontispiece: Hot Pursuit.

On the title page: Grave Digger, the notorious panel van-
bodied monster.

On the back cover: Monster truck nostalgia racing: Bigfoot 1
makes an exhibition appearance at the 2000 Spring Jamboree.

Printed in China

CONTENTS

Such a monster has, then, really existence!
I cannot doubt it, yet I am lost in surprise and admiration.
—Mary Shelley, Frankenstein *(1818)*

ACKNOWLEDGMENTS

This book wouldn't have happened without many helping hands and brains. First and foremost, Ken Brubaker and his in-the-trenches photos were the catalyst. He and his family are some of the biggest fans of monster trucks. Next, Chad Caruthers and the Motorbooks staff gave us carte blanche—we've tried not to hang ourselves on the long leash.

For certain, former and current coworkers shaped the finished product. Chronologically, Robin Hartfiel and Greg Brown provided entrée to this racket. *Four Wheeler* colleagues Liz and John Stewart gave a kid a job. Stuart Bourdon, Bruce W. Smith, Willie Worthy, and Jimmy "Bud Miller" Nylund showed me the ropes. Granville King instilled style and elegance, both at the typewriter and behind the wheel (but not necessarily in the passenger's seat). Kudos also go to Jim Ryan for his efforts to elevate the four-wheel drive enthusiast-mag biz. Special commendations to Leonard Emanuelson and Jim McGowan of Automedia 2000 for tolerating tardiness during this project.

Duane Elliott deserves his own sentences. No one on the planet consistently puts his camera lenses closer to flying trucks, and Duane has unashamedly communicated the phenomenon to the masses for 20 years now. His vision has made the publishing side of the 4x4 industry quantum amounts more fun. Frank "Big Dummy" Schettini is always generous with his time and talents (and tolerance of little nieces and nephews playing on his trucks). A true original, Frank is one of the rare people who consistently converts wacky ideas into realities. Ben "Smoky Burn-Out" Stewart, of *Popular Mechanics,* generously let me plunder his reference library and shared insights as one of the few civilians to ever drive Bigfoot. Others include Ned Bacon and Rick and Laura Péwé, who'll be embarrassed to have their names in this book because it isn't about Jeeps.

The human ring-and-pinions of monster machinery also helped create this book. The Bigfoot family—Bob, Marilyn, and Penny Chandler; Scott Johnston; and all of the drivers and crew—naturally is the foundation of the sport. The informative "Monsters Monthly" column on TruckWorld.com, by Eric Stern and Dave and Bev Huntoon, was a vital resource. Marty Garza, of Overkill Racing, was the source of endless technical information. Thanks, too, to various promoters for their assistance, particularly C. Bruce Hubley and Doc Riley, of Special Events.

Finally, thanks to Mom and Dad (who stocked the house with books), brother Steve, and sister Cindy.

CHAPTER 1

THE CONCEPTION
RURAL ROCK STARS

We're five-wide in the sleeper cab, with the driver and copilot in the air-suspended bucket seats. The trailer was abandoned at the fairgrounds, and seven of us are en route to dinner. The stickers on the tractor's doors say Bigfoot 4x4. Our chauffeur is a professional driver. In addition to holding a commercial driver's license, Dan Runte is one of a handful of people on the planet who holds a Monster Truck Racing Association (MTRA) license. At that time, an MTRA license was rarer than the certification required to fly an F/A-18 Hornet.

At work, Dan normally drives alone. I normally walk to a restaurant that's within an Opie Taylor sidearm rock sling of the motel. But a chainlink fence separates the motel and restaurant parking lots. The seven of us who are crammed in the Bigfoot tractor all work in the automotive industry as mechanics, enthusiast-magazine page fillers, and pro drivers. Photographer Ken Brubaker's wallet even includes a commercial driver's license in front of his Nikon Professional Services card. Because we all owe our paychecks to internal combustion, walking somehow seems heretical this night, though seven people in a diesel pusher should qualify as an environmentally conscious carpool. More important, Dan has the keys to the Bigfoot transport rig, and this is a once-in-a-lifetime opportunity.

We drive one block. Seven motley men spill out of the trailerless tractor and into the parking lot. In the restaurant/bar, we squeeze into a booth. We haven't had time to scrutinize the menu when it happens: A young lady in her late teens or early twenties approaches our booth. She shyly asks, "Excuse me, but are y'all with Bigfoot?" Without hesitation, one of the five of us whose paycheck is signed by Bob and Marilyn Chandler replies, "We sure are. Do you have tickets for the show tomorrow?"

She sighs. "I have to work, but I'm trying to get off early."

Two tickets appear immediately from one of the five. "Bring a friend." Odds are she will.

This is *Almost Famous* a decade before the movie's release. For certain, the scene above would be much more dramatic if this book were adapted for the big screen. Produced on a Roger Corman B-movie budget to ensure a blue-collar tone, it'd be titled *Clubfoot* to avoid paying licensing fees to Bigfoot. Obviously, the "C" in the *Clubfoot* logo is in a gimpy typeface.

In the movie version, the Clubfoot crew travels in a multi-rig convoy. Team Clubfoot has a separate hospitality trailer in addition to the truck-transport rig. Club Clubfoot—as the rolling suite is known—has a dance floor, DJ booth, stage, buffet spread; a big-screen

Don Runte as Snakebite driver "Colt Cobra" in 1994. *Tom Morr*

television that plays nonstop motorsports; plus bolted-to-the-walls racing seats. Has-been actors, the caliber of whom did cameos on *Love Boat* or the *Cannonball Run* movies, schmooze in the trailer as the convoy travels cross-country between events. Dressed in embroidered racing team-style shirts, these working-for-scale actors portray monster truck show promoters, rival drivers, and the Clubfoot team's corporate sponsors.

Every item in the hospitality trailer has a sponsor and is tagged with at least one decal. For example, the mirrored disco ball suspended from the roof carries a wheel polish company's logo. Dom DeLuise's shirt sports patches from frozen-food companies and grocery store chains. Jerry Reed, wearing a Coors cap (assuming the brewer is willing to pay the producer a product-placement fee), reprises his Snowman character from

Mike Vaters and his Black Stallion 2000 helped redefine the sport's freestyle feature. At the 1997 New England Jamboree, Vaters fell prey to a five-feet deep pit.

Smokey and the Bandit. But this time, he's Plowman to avoid having to pay royalties to Hal Needham. Reed drives the rig as long as his log book legally allows, then moves to the trailer, straps on his guitar, and takes the Club Clubfoot stage. At the mic, he lip-synchs catchy country songs about the trials and tribulations of the vagabond monster truck driver. These ballads are penned and performed by up-and-coming country stars, because the budget won't cover Jerry Reed originals. Incidental music is supplied—for a percentage of any soundtrack sales—by old college buddies who are now in the real-life Clubfoot Orchestra.

An over-the-road reception isn't without its foibles. Just as airline pilots foreshadow turbulence by turning

Bigfoot's first-ever charity event was in 1979 at the Muscle Power Truck-A-Thon Muscular Dystrophy fundraiser in Illinois. The 5-ton truck stood 8 feet, 6 inches tall at the time and sported dual 48-inch tires per corner for the event. *Bigfoot 4x4, Inc.*

Bigfoot driver Jim Kramer did the first "record jump" at the 1987 Fall Jamboree. Dan Runte set the current record of 202 feet over a Boeing 747 in 1999. *Bigfoot 4x4, Inc.*

on the seatbelt sign, the rig's driver blasts the "ooga" airhorn to indicate potholed pavement ahead. When this warning sounds, the party takes a hiatus, with club occupants scurrying to the racing seats and strapping themselves in with five-point harnesses. The camera lingers on Adrienne Barbeau as she adjusts her harness's shoulder straps, an underwire-bra company's sticker plainly visible on her shirt at all times.

Burt Reynolds, wearing the Hair Therapy Institute custom-embroidered shirt, plays the amoral antagonistic promoter who plots to be the Vince McMahon of the world. Wilford Brimley is the bearded, Bob Chandler-like protagonist and Clubfoot owner. He donates a portion of each show's proceeds to children's funds.

The Clubfoot truck is a show unto itself. Three of its tires are the requisite 66-inch tundra fare, but the

driver's side rear is only a 60-incher. The truck's name obviously comes from its askew stance. To help compensate for this genetic flaw, Clubfoot is outfitted with the finest in East Los Angeles-style hydraulics. This technology allows Clubfoot's body to "dance" side to side and front to rear. For exhibition runs, the driver walks alongside the truck with a remote-control switch panel in hand. Clubfoot bounces up to the row of junk cars then proceeds to hop over them like a 1966 Impala in a Snoop Dogg video—only with six-feet-tall farm-implement tires instead of 50-series rubber wraparound wire wheels. The crowd goes wild, spontaneously combusting into aerobics-studio dance moves as unintelligible hip-hop music with thundering bass blasts from the stadium's sound system.

Ian Ziering portrays Clubfoot's suave yet big-hearted driver. Adorned in a shirt that bears a large American Chiropractor's Alliance patch, Ziering is a fan-favorite, good-guy driver who stays after every show until the last autograph is signed and every baby is kissed. Reynolds attempts to convert Ziering to the dark side by promising him the commissionership of the mega monster truck monopoly once Reynolds achieves his global big-truck motorsports domination.

Zany madcap adventures ensue, with scenes inspired by the Bob Hope/Bing Crosby road movies and big-rig stunt sequences choreographed by Hal Needham's most-affordable nephew. But enough of the fictional version of life on the circuit.

The reality of covering these shows is closer to *Almost Famous* character William Miller's life or Cameron Crowe's real stint as a *Rolling Stone* writer who travels with rock bands. Prior to hanging out with the Bigfoot crew, I thought that the human cogs in the monster truck machinery were closer to circus carnies than rock stars in the sociological strata. Once a part of this world-class entertainment posse, I now know why so many people have attempted to build and campaign monster trucks: These are larger than life rock stars—rural rock stars.

One of the 4x4 world's biggest challenges is cresting the Big Elim pea-gravel hill at Gravelrama in Cleves, Ohio. Bob Chandler joined the exclusive "Over the Hill Club" in 1985. *Bigfoot 4x4, Inc.*

Way bigger than Dolly Parton ever was, Bigfoot is arguably the Dave Matthews Band of American motorsports. NASCAR might be the automotive equivalent of the Rolling Stones, but the Pettys and Waltrips of the world won't soon appear at a stadium or fairgrounds near you. Bigfoot will, though.

After dinner, we adjourn to the restaurant's pool tables. The locals swarm us. They ask, "Which one of you drives Bigfoot?" Little do they (or I, for that matter) know that Dan Runte not only drives Bigfoot as well as the transport tractor, but he'll go on to become the greatest driver of all time. How many humans are in the second decade of dominating their respective sport with no end in sight?

Back at the hotel bar later that night, more townies gravitate toward Dan. Men want to know about Bigfoot. What's it like to crush cars with 66-inch tires? How is driving a monster truck different from four-wheeling in lifted pickups that roll on 40- to 44-inch tires? Women lean forward to hear Dan so that they can tell their friends they met a celebrity. Like roadies for rock stars, the rest of the Bigfoot crew hangs out while Dan unassumingly holds court. A version of this scenario happens at every motel that has a Bigfoot rig parked in its lot.

Few motorsports fans understand the power behind this phenomenon. Something that started as a publicity stunt in the 1970s has grown into an international spectacle. Monster trucks have mutated from a 4x4 shop on the outskirts of St. Louis into a punchline on late-night talk shows. Their rise in popularity has been as wild as these 5-ton machines' one-wheeled landings after clearing a row of junked cars. The origins of these machines, their evolution, and the future of this unique portion of Americana are all vital parts of monster truck mania.

State-of-the-art in 1987: Bigfoot 3 sported a square-channel frame, front-mounted Boss 429 engine, and an early multi-link suspension at this show in Long Beach, California. *Bigfoot 4x4, Inc.*

CHAPTER 2

EMBRYONIC STAGE
BIG FOOT 1

Blame it on Alaska. Originally known as "The Icebox" and "Seward's Folly" when U.S. Secretary of State William Seward masterminded the Alaska Purchase from Russia in 1867 for $7.2 million, this transaction has turned out to be one of the best real-estate deals of all time. Most people are well aware of Alaska's vast natural resources and its strategic value during the cold war. However, few know that the seeds of monster truckdom were fertilized here.

The year was 1968. Bob Chandler, a carpenter/contractor and automotive enthusiast from St. Louis took his family on a three-month Alaska vacation. He'd outfitted his 1967 Ford F-250 4x4 pickup with a camper. However, the truck's tires weren't tough enough to handle the Alcan Highway. Bob relied on local knowledge to find tires tough enough to conquer the Alcan and then hold up for the return trip to Missouri.

The experience changed Bob's life—and ultimately helped make the Ford F-Series pickup truck the best-selling vehicle in America. Long before the St. Louis Rams achieved success in the Midwest, Bob and Marilyn Chandler stumbled onto something that would eventually energize the automotive industry and become a pop-culture icon worldwide.

Following the Alaska vacation, Bob continued to customize cars and trucks, a hobby he had adopted in high school. The Chandlers also enjoyed exploring the back roads through the outlying woodlands of their area. Bob and his friend Jim Kramer (who was also a partner in a winter snow-removal service) would take out their 4x4s and purposely look for sticky predicaments. Broken parts often resulted from pushing their 4x4s to "go where no truck had gone before." Bob began upgrading his own 1967 truck to meet the challenges. Soon, the handful of other local 4x4 owners took note of Bob's innovations and asked him to upgrade their trucks. The carport at the Chandler residence became cluttered with "needs fixin'" 4x4s. Around the same time, Bob had a nasty motorcycle accident that forced him to give up the construction business. Judging by their own driveway, the Chandlers recognized a need for a 4x4 parts and service business. In 1974, the Chandlers opened Midwest Four Wheel Drive Center in Hazelwood, Missouri.

The Birth of Bigfoot

One of Bob Chandler's first moves was to buy a new 1974 F-250 4x4. This truck became a laboratory for parts and engineering experiments. Oversized, Alaska-influenced 1200x/6.5 tires were one of the first modifications. The taller the truck grew, the more attention it attracted for Midwest Four Wheel Drive. Bob and Jim

Monster truck nostalgia racing: Bigfoot 1 makes an exhibition appearance at the 2000 Spring Jamboree.

continued to flog the truck off-road, upgrading it every time a part broke. Bob's aggressive behind-the-wheel escapades prompted Midwest's general manager, Ron Magruder, to nickname him "Bigfoot." Recognizing a good pun when they heard one, Chandler and his crew attached the name to the truck in 1976.

Bigfoot was an instant local legend. Bob was curious to see how his big truck would be received outside of the St. Louis area. In 1977, he attempted to enter a show in Las Vegas. However, Bob's application was rejected based on the vehicle being a 1974 F-250—not exactly a custom or classic car. Bob drove Bigfoot to Vegas anyway. Parked outside of the show, Bigfoot attracted more attention than the cars inside. The promoters recognized the truck's show-stopping capability and promptly moved Bigfoot inside.

By 1979, the tables had turned. Word of mouth about this tall truck was such that Bigfoot became a paid attraction. The Chandlers' first for-profit gig was at a car show in Denver. Media coverage let the proverbial genie out of the bottle, and the Chandlers wasted no time figuratively uncorking the headers and putting the pedal to the medal. Within months, Bob and his Ford were making exhibition appearances at truck events.

In 1981, Bigfoot went big-time. Moviegoers had a chance to see it on the big screen for the first time in *Take This Job and Shove It*. The movie's best parts are Johnny Paycheck's theme song and Bigfoot's scenes.

Car-Crushing

Light-duty pickup trucks lost their innocence in March 1981. Bob Chandler had seen someone drive a big-tire pickup onto a car's front bumper. Always wanting to go bigger and better, Bob set up a stunt in a field near the Midwest shop. He drove Bigfoot over some junked cars and captured the feat on videotape. Copies of the tape circulated among 4x4 fans, and Bigfoot instantly catapulted to mythical status in enthusiast circles.

Bobby Chandler wasn't quite as tall as Bigfoot's 48-inch tires in 1979. The front pushbar proves that Bigfoot 1 also served as the Midwest shop truck. *Bigfoot 4x4, Inc.*

The first "Bigfoot" in 1945 stood one-foot, eight-inches tall. Its top speed with Bob Chandler pushing (as shown here) was reportedly 6 miles per hour—downhill. *Bigfoot 4x4, Inc.*

A local promoter caught wind of crushing and persuaded Bob to recreate the stunt at a local racetrack. Not all motorsports fans could relate to driving counterclockwise in circles as fast as possible, but all motorists who've ever been stuck in gridlock traffic responded with primordial emotion upon seeing Bigfoot drive over cars. Motorsports had been altered forever.

Car-crushing took off during the mid-1980s. Truck owners—ranging from retired contractors to recently licensed 16-year-olds—lifted their rigs, fitted oversized tires and wheels, and drove over any inanimate object that would impress their friends and family. (This foreshadowed the alliance between wrestling and monster trucks—amateur crushing appealed to the same people who staged and attended impromptu wrestling shows more than a decade before "backyard wrestling" videos were produced.)

Monster truck exhibitions became sideshows during truck pulls and mud races. But as rodeo clowns often overshadow the cowboys and Brahma bulls, monster trucks stole the show from sled-pulling pickups and tractors. In fact, a 1983 exhibition crush by Bigfoot at the Pontiac Silverdome in Detroit incited a near riot. Event promoter Bob George described the spectacle shortly after the fact. "We first booked monster trucks at the Silverdome during a tractor pull. A truck [Bigfoot] came out of the tunnel, crawled over four cars, and then had to be escorted off the floor because 50,000 people came over the rails to get closer." Following a lengthy flashbulb frenzy, Chandler and Bigfoot escaped unscathed—for the time being.

Bigfoot was still street legal at that point, and Bob drove it to and from shows. After the Silverdome show, George Carpenter, the promoter's event director (and

By 1980, Bigfoot had new meats, a chromed bumper, the soon-to-be-famous logo, and "F880" badging. It was also still street legal. *Bigfoot 4x4, Inc.*

subsequent builder of the Megasaurus car-eating fire-breather) remembered pulling in to the motel as Bigfoot was pulling out. Thinking that Chandler was going to dinner, Carpenter followed the big Ford. Pulling alongside, Carpenter realized that some young punk had stolen Bigfoot and was going for a joyride! Carpenter gave chase until the kid eventually lost control, crashed Bigfoot, and fled on foot. The battered Ford was loaded on a trailer for transport back to St. Louis. That crazy day in Detroit is generally considered the debut of monster trucks as marquee performers.

Promoters obviously realized that monster trucks—not tractor pullers or mud boggers—deserved top billing. Jim Kramer cemented this status in 1986. At a show in Indianapolis, Kramer hit the junkers, lost control, and endoed the 15,000-pound truck across the Hoosier Dome's (now the RCA Dome) infield. Fans went ballistic. ESPN aired the footage for the masses.

As time went on, monster trucks gained and maintained their popularity. As we approach the 30th anniversary of Bigfoot 1, this uniquely American mechanical phenomenon thunders on. A common punchline for "white trash" jokes, monster trucks continue to evoke an emotional response from humans of all types and ages. Regardless of whether we laugh at them or with them, monster trucks remain larger than life.

Powered by a 571-cubic inch Ford big-block, Ms. Bigfoot was the world's first minitruck-bodied mini-monster. Marilyn Chandler introduced the truck in 1985, becoming the world's first female monster driver in the process. *Bigfoot 4x4, Inc.*

CHAPTER 3

INFANCY
WEANING AND TEETHING

The 1980s might go down in history as the decade of bad hairstyles—and of the monster truck. No, these two aren't mutually exclusive. Eight-ton mechanical marvels captured the psyches of kids, their parents, and even grandparents throughout the world. Hollywood wasted no time in casting these machines. In addition to *Take This Job and Shove It,* Bigfoot alone appeared in these movies: *Cannonball Run 2* (1982), *Police Academy 2* (1985), *Police Academy 6* (1989), *Road House* (1989), and *Tango & Cash* (1989).

Homegrown monster trucks began to spread faster than Great Lakes-region rust. Mud racers and truck and tractor pullers were the first groups of gearheads to get caught up in the monster frenzy. Monster truck exhibition runs stole the show from the mudders and pullers. These competitors realized that living in the limelight meant going big. Sure, the top tractor pullers boasted as many as five big-buck, all-aluminum, $50,000-a-pop Rodeck engines, and Art Arfons' Green Monster tractor wowed crowds with its fire-shooting jet engine, but for pure entertainment value, these impressive machines were no match for the new breed of stock-bodied pickup trucks on grotesquely oversized tires.

Instead of chastising these Bigfoot knockoffs, Bob Chandler embraced the competition. After all, he built Midwest Four Wheel Drive by creating the biggest, toughest trucks in the business. The fact that monster trucks have survived as long as they have is a testament to Chandler's progressive thinking and constant quest to find the next level of performance. Besides, heroes emerge from adversity.

Bigfoot's first formidable foe was the USA-1 Chevy/GMC. Builder/owner Everett Jasmer would lay claim to many innovations, and the competition undoubtedly pushed the red Bow-Tie and big Blue Oval to attempt to outdo one another on literally a weekly basis. Best of all, the Ford/Chevy rivalry filled the grandstands.

Other trucks began to carve their impressions in American psyches. Exotic animal trainer/former drag racer Fred Shafer birthed the Bear Foot Chevy at his Pontoon Beach, Illinois, shop and wild animal preserve. Throughout the 1980s and 1990s, Fred consistently performed at the sport's upper echelon, most notably while flying the Dodge colors.

The fourth founding father of monster trucks is Jack Willman. He and son Jackie entered the tall-truck fray in the 1980s and remained mainstays until the Taurus team was sold to Paul "Monster Patrol" Shafer a few years ago.

The common denominator among the first-generation builders and drivers was unassuming personalities. Most were hardworking Midwesterners

Hercules prepares for a landing at the 1996 Spring Jamboree Nationals.

who chose to express themselves through their mechanical creations. These men tended to be camera shy, in stark contrast to their trucks. For one of the few times in the history of competitive internal combustion, the machines garnered more attention than the people who created and drove them.

Grave Digger Unearthed

Every successful industry has its share of insane geniuses who don't accept "business as usual." These against-the-grain individuals revitalize their vocation—and often become cult heroes in the process. Apple Computers accomplished this in the 1980s, proving that IBM and other companies grossly underestimated the personal-computer market. History might remember Apple's Steve Jobs and Steve Wozniak as world-changers.

About the same time that the first Macintosh computers were being assembled in a northern California garage, a beast from the southeast was born. In 1981, Dennis Anderson cobbled together a mud-racing truck from junked-vehicle spare parts in a Virginia chicken coop. A real-life tribute to the Johnny Cash anthem "One Piece at a Time," Anderson's truck was more or less a clapped-out 1951 Ford pickup, but it was powered by a high-performance Chevy engine.

Dennis and his ragtag truck didn't get much respect at their first mud races. Tired of taking competitors' verbal abuse based on his truck's appearance, Dennis defended himself with the now-immortal line, "I'll take this old junk and dig your grave." Grave Digger was out of the womb.

Circumstance and fluke are often the mothers of opportunity. When a monster truck didn't make an exhibition appearance at a 1984 mud race, Dennis and his what-the-hell attitude filled the void. He crushed cars in his by-then panel-van bodied mud-racing truck, and the crowd went berserk. Dennis put two and two together, got 4x4, and gave monster truckdom a high-octane shot in the arm.

In 1991, Wayne Smozaneck's Tropical Thunder was a basic big Chevy. The pair later gained fame in Special Events Penda Poins series.

Featuring its now-signature graveyard graphics by Fred Bumann, Grave Digger hit the circuit full-time in 1988. Fans immediately embraced its classic bodylines and airbrushed side-panel art. Dennis' hyper-aggressive driving style endeared Grave Digger to fans even further. Few drivers have crashed as hard as often as Dennis has in Grave Digger. Best of all, Dennis and "Digger" are still flogging as strong as ever—unlike other drivers who've succumbed to back problems or a common kidney ailment known in the business as "leaky faucet."

Chassis Master: Dan Patrick

The roots of monster trucks are firmly planted in the American Heartland. This history of farm sports is beyond the scope of this book, but "agricultural engineers" competed against each other in work-related challenges way before the internal-combustion engine was invented. Ox- and mule-team shootouts were the precursors to modern-day truck and tractor pulling and mud racing.

Most of monster truckdom's movers and shapers cut their gear teeth in mud racing or pulling. Dan Patrick is one who came from the pulling side of the fairgrounds. A pro puller at age 17, Dan built his first competitive tractor in 1973. He's credited with creating the first dragster-style puller in 1987.

A year after unveiling his "diggerster" puller, Dan bought the Samson monster truck. His knack for technical innovation astounded the industry. In fact, Dan helped propel monster trucks from their sideshow-exhibition status to full-blown motorsports competitors. He was instrumental in developing Bigfoot 8, the first tube-framed truck, in 1989.

Dan remains at the forefront of chassis technology. His frames are the current state-of-the-sport. As of 2003, some 55 monster trucks had been built on Dan's frames, and he has orders pending for several others. He's also

Longtime driver turned television commentator Scott Stephens initially rose to prominence in the fat-framed King Krunch. Scott's other creations include the jet-powered Silver Bullet truck, built in the late 1980s.

For many, the late 1980s and early 1990s were the glory days of monster trucks. Average Joes took actual sheet-metal bodies and mounted them over squared-tubed frames and Terra tires.

First-generation trucks weighed up to 20,000 pounds. They had thick steel frames, radically arched leaf springs, and multiple shocks per wheel. This AM/PM truck currently hangs on the wall at the Petersen Museum in Los Angeles. *Frank Schettini/Monster Jerky*

built at least 14 complete monster trucks. But Dan isn't strictly an under-the-skin wizard.

Through his work with the Bigfoot team, Dan was at the cutting edge of what became known as "3-D" body styles. Expanding on the Grave Digger approach to unique (non-factory 4x4) bodylines, Bigfoot's

Snakebite introduced bulbous, wacky, fiberglass skin to the monster world. Dan Patrick promptly humanized the 3-D body in 1993 when he added bodybuilder-look arms to Samson's fenders as part of a promotional deal with the *American Gladiators* television show. He patented this design in 1997.

35

CHAPTER 4

ADOLESCENCE
TESTOSTERONE/TECHNOLOGY

In the early days of monsterdom, size was all that mattered. Shortly after Bigfoot 1 stood on 48-inch tires in the mid-1970s, legions of bandwagoneers tried to figure out how to make their trucks even taller than the blue Ford. A popular early method was to obtain military-surplus 2–1/2-ton axles and farm-implement tires, then adapt these to a standard pickup-truck chassis.

Unfortunately, the military axles made the stock pickup-truck frame the weak link. Backyard "Bubba" engineering of the era didn't account for the increased torsional/twisting stresses these big axles transferred to the frame. At the time, few builders had a firm understanding of physics or suspension dynamics. As car-crushing became the rage, many a monster's frame snapped under the hard impact of a post-launch landing.

Good ol' American ingenuity was applied to the problem: Conventional wisdom seems to dictate that bigger is always better and that heavier must mean stronger. Monster builders noted the weak (and tweak) points and reinforced their frames accordingly by welding on extra pieces of steel plate. C-channel frames were fully enclosed (boxed) for rigidity. This approach often proved to be a Band-Aid fix—the stress point simply moved past the reinforcement.

Frame stresses increased as tire sizes and axle weight grew. When 66-inch tires and 5-ton military axles became the standard competitive setup, many monster builders supplemented their trucks' factory chassis with custom subframes. The theory was that if one frame couldn't handle the load, then a second one welded to it should double chassis strength. This approach rarely accounted for torsional loads. Also, overall vehicle weight wasn't seen as a factor.

The next evolutionary step was born more of convenience than technology. Realizing that military frames were designed to handle the axles mounted underneath them, monster builders figured that adapting a pickup body to a military-style vehicle made more sense than transplanting military underpinnings to a light-duty truck. The straight-frame era was launched.

This design solved some of the strength issues but created new challenges: to fit the truck body and driveline, extensive frame modifications (including shortening the wheelbase, adding crossmembers, and fabricating body, engine, and transmission mounts) still had to be executed. Instead of cutting and pasting around an existing frame, some builders decided to start from scratch. Fabricating a custom chassis from either C-channel or box tubing allowed monster builders to mount driveline components at their most advantageous locations. Also, crossmembers in these ladder-style chassis became integrated into the underlying structure instead of being

Dungeon of Doom was one of the most menacing of the 3-D trucks. Few people remember that it was originally tied to a WCW wrestler.

Bigfoot 10 without its body. The space-frame design protects the driver by supporting the vehicle's 9,500-pound weight from all sides.

slapped-on afterthoughts. These heavy frames typically were made from at least 1/4-inch thick mild- or high-tensile steel, and the rails were often between 8 and 12 inches tall. These straight frames were constructed for strength, their trade-off being extraordinary weight—some early monsters tipped the scales at close to 20,000 pounds.

Fat Ain't Where It's At

The inception of side-by-side racing in 1987 caused monster truckers to reevaluate their designs. Competition made overall weight an important safety issue. Foremost, heavier objects in motion take longer to stop than lighter ones. Also, bed-mounted roll bars couldn't support the truck's weight when it flipped. The solution was race car-style in-cab roll cages with numerous spreaders (kicker bars) to distribute stresses more evenly. These improvements and other safety concerns prompted Bob Chandler to create the Monster Truck Racing Association (MTRA). Monster trucks were now becoming less like the pickups on car dealers' lots and more like oval-track race cars.

The structural integrity provided by these triangulated (spreading stress over a series of triangles) roll cages was a major breakthrough. The main frame rails no longer had to absorb all the stress, so smaller, lighter material—as small as 3-inch square or round tubing—could be used. Mounting brackets for suspension and

MTRA: DEDICATED TO MONSTER TRUCK SAFETY

One of Bob Chandler's most visionary contributions to exhibition motorsports was forming the Monster Truck Racing Association (MTRA). Realizing that event promoters are more focused on ticket sales and corporate sponsorships than on vehicle specifications, Chandler decided that owners and drivers had to be responsible for their own safety. Spectator preservation was also a paramount concern.

By 1987, monster racing was kicking into high gear. Chandler invited 11 truck owners and drivers to help him draft guidelines that would help ensure the sport's future. In December 1987, 49 truck owners and drivers assembled at Bigfoot headquarters to formally create the MTRA.

Today, most shows put on by national promoters adhere to MTRA guidelines. All MTRA-sanctioned trucks must pass annual inspections to ensure their mechanical integrity. The vehicle checklist has more than 100 requirements. Certified MTRA truck inspectors are monster mechanics, builders, owners, and drivers who've undergone a technical-training program and passed a test. They must be recertified every year.

The MTRA also elects a member to represent the organization with the SFI Foundation, an association that was established to issue and administer standards for racing equipment. The SFI works with parts and accessories manufacturers, as well as racing organizations, to establish safety parameters for race-stressed components. Parts that are typically monitored include transmission scattershields, supercharger restraint blankets, fuel cells, fire extinguishers, helmets, and harnesses. The SFI classifies MTRA-certified monster trucks in the same category as other professional race vehicles and organizations such as the NHRA (National Hot Rod Association), IRL (Indy Racing League), SCCA (Sports Car Club of America), and IMCA (International Motor Contest Association).

All drivers must pass rigorous testing to qualify for MTRA certification—a competitive monster truck driver's license. Completing classroom training earns drivers a Class B MTRA license, the equivalent of a learner's permit. To get the full Class A competition license, a driver must safely compete in 10 sanctioned races.

One of the MTRA's largest accomplishments is requiring all trucks to have a remote ignition interrupter. If a driver should lose control of the truck, the event's safety official can "kill" the monster's engine with a remote-control switch. This has prevented trucks from leaving the competition area on a few occasions. MTRA requirements also call for all drivers to wear a five-point safety harness, a helmet, a neck collar, gloves, and a fire-retardant suit. All MTRA-certified trucks must have an approved onboard fire-retardant system, and each vehicle must also have a minimum 2.5-pound fire extinguisher within the driver's reach.

Although a few unfortunate accidents have gravely injured spectators and event personnel, no monster truck driver has ever been seriously injured. The MTRA is dedicated to ensuring that the sport remains safe for everyone involved.

driveline components could be incorporated into the overall design. This minimized the severe angles that led to numerous broken parts in the older, fat-framed trucks. Suspension design evolved from the factory-pickup-style leaf springs to four-link style—parallel bars attached to the axles and frame with pivoting joints allowed the axles to articulate more than the older springs. The result is that the tires spent more time on firm surfaces and fewer milliseconds airborne.

A logical extension of race-style triangulation was tubular frames. Bob Chandler debuted Bigfoot 8 with this setup in 1989. Possibly even more impressive than the frame itself was the fact that Chandler and Dan Patrick used computer-aided design (CAD), making

Another view of Bigfoot 10 nude: Visible components include 66-inch Firestones, a tube-frame Dan Patrick chassis, nitro shocks, onboard fire-extinguishing system, and a mid-engine Ford big-block. *Bigfoot 4x4, Inc.*

Bigfoot 8 one of the first trucks to be conceived on an electronic machine instead of on a shop floor. These new-age skeletons were similar to Winston Cup cars' and were made from 2-inch diameter, .120-inch wall-thickness tubing with integrated roll cages. These days, most modern monsters' chassis are designed using Auto CAD.

Tubular space frames, in which the frame and roll cage function as a single unit, also improved safety by lowering the monster trucks' center of gravity (CG). Lower means more stable. The farther down the drive-train components can be mounted in the frame, the easier the truck is to control. In a one- or two-point landing after a jump, the lower the weight is located in the truck, the faster control returns.

Suspension

Monster trucks became popular immediately, because, with the exception of the tires, they resembled an off-the-assembly-line pickup. Leaf springs attached the axles to the frame, just like your job-site-variety pickup. The primary difference was that the monster truck springs had more of a "V" to their arc than light-duty pickups' in order to help the body clear the large tires. In addition to custom leaf springs, early monster trucks used long brackets that stuck down below the frame to mount the springs, and they often employed steel blocks between the axles and springs for even more suspension lift.

The springs were stiff. Their steep arc came at the expense of flexibility. The leafpacks kept the axles firmly

Bigfoot's suspension is tunable by varying the mounting location of its upper 4-link bars.

Nitrogen-charged shocks allow monster trucks to travel on gas.

in place, and the resulting buckboard effect took its toll on many monster drivers' vertebrae. Traction bars—which keep the axles in place by limiting their ability to rotate as the springs move up and down—were a slight improvement. Modern technology was incorporated when traction bars were outfitted with hydraulic cylinders to absorb some of the stress and allow the springs to compress more easily. The result was improved suspension travel—the axles' ability to move up and down.

Another suspension reality is that the springs only support the weight above them. The heaviest parts of a monster truck—the tires, wheels, and axles—must be controlled by shock absorbers. Unfortunately for builders, other forms of motorsports offered little help

in this area, because the standard race vehicle's engine, frame, and body outweigh its axles, tires, and wheels. Innovation was necessary.

Again, bigger was the knee-jerk engineering solution. After all, more weight must require more shocks, right? But more shocks mean more force required to compress the dampers, so we're back to the stiff suspension that hypothetically rides like Fred Flintstone's rock-tired car. Custom-4x4 builders jumped on this bandwagon. By the late 1980s, a truck owner's self-esteem was apparently proportional to the number of shocks he could mount on his pickup. Embarrassingly, neon-colored shock boots apparently earned extra points with the ladies.

Monster trucks get approximately 1 mile per 5 gallons of methanol race fuel.

Mechanical Darwinism provoked minor strides in suspension design. Somebody apparently looked under a 1970's Cadillac Fleetwood to see why it absorbed train tracks like a down comforter engulfs an infant. The "secret" was long leaf springs that had a less-radical arch. So the V-springs began to disappear, replaced by longer, kinder, and gentler leaf packs. Marty Garza, of Overkill Racing, recalled that prime examples of these setups allowed as much as 12 inches of up-and-down axle movement.

Leaf-spring suspensions had another drawback, however: Each spring works independently. In the unfortunate event of a one-point landing, the axle deflects rearward on the impact side of the truck but might stay centered in the wheel well on the opposite end. The truck then pulls to the side with the compressed spring. This isn't beneficial in racing, where the one who finds the fastest route between points A and B gets the trophy.

Race-prepped Bigfoot trucks use German ZF axles. Originally intended for industrial forklifts, they're modified for monster purposes.

Bigfoot's 1,500 horsepower comes from a 571-cubic inch Ford V-8 that's force-fed air by an 8-71 BDS supercharger.

The farther a 15,000-pound object gets off-track, the longer it takes to correct its path.

4-Links

The final (or at least current) evolution in suspension design is the 4-link system. Its main advantage is that it separates the functions of axle location and weight support.

The 4-link uses a pair of parallel bars to connect the end of each axle to the truck's frame. This keeps the axles perpendicular to the frame, eliminating leaf springs' tendency to make the truck "dart" to the most-compressed side.

Early 4-link designs often had a shorter upper arm. This was a packaging necessity in order to clear drivetrain parts. However, this meant that the bars in each pair didn't deflect at the same rate—shades of sloppy leaf-spring handling. As engineering evolved, frames were designed so that each link rod could be the same length, improving stability and making handling more predictable.

However, the truck's weight still had to be supported. Since the 4-link kept the axle under control, some monster builders drafted their old leaf springs into weight-control duties. Mounting the springs with pivotable shackles at each end permitted the leaf packs to compress and rebound without adversely affecting axle positioning.

Another option was air bags. Made of thick rubber, these bags replaced the leaf springs, mounting between the axle and frame. Pumped-up air bags lifted the truck higher, and deflating the bags lowered the ride height. Air bags saved weight compared to leaf springs, but they still limited up-and-down suspension travel to about 12 inches.

A third option proved to be the best. Like air bags, coil springs could handle weight-bearing duties in tighter quarters than leaf packs. Spring stiffness and ride height could be engineered into the spring by varying the thickness and overall height of the coiled steel.

Coil-Overs

Motorcycle engineering is often years ahead of corresponding four-wheeled technological advances. In a way, the 4-link is the automotive version of a motorcycle's swing-arm suspension.

Monster truck racing proved early on that the winning truck was usually the one whose tires contacted *terra firma* (or *junkus carus*) the most. Off-road racers had known this since the 1960s. Vehicles whose bodies stayed parallel to the ground while the suspension systems gyrated up and down often won. And when they didn't, their drivers often had less blood in their urine at the finish line, because their kidneys hadn't been jostled into submission by rigid suspensions.

Since off-road racing was the only other motorsport in which vehicles consistently go airborne, attempt to land under control, then reapply engine power to the ground through the tires, engineers cribbed a few notes from the Baja racers. Shock absorbers were the key area. Until the late 1980s, they were also a limiting factor. The longest over-the-counter truck shock only had about 12 inches of piston travel.

Then, the tunable, rebuildable race shock hit the market. Designed by Lance King for the Kuster company, these shocks featured massive 3-inch-diameter bodies and could be built with an 18-inch-stroke piston rod to break the 12-inch suspension-travel barrier. Desert racers even cut holes in their pickup beds to fit the longest-stroke-possible shocks.

These race shocks had other best-of-all-worlds features. Introduced in the early 1990s, they were user-rebuildable and tunable—swapping discs inside the shock body or dialing an external knob regulated fluid flow to soften or stiffen the damping action. The shocks also included pads for extra cost to accommodate coil springs over their bodies (a $1,000 option per shock at the time), allowing ride-height adjustability and solving many space concerns. Rebuildable

Bob Chandler launched the hybrid van/tank Bigfoot FasTrax at the Indianapolis Jamboree in 1987. Its lack of suspension made for a brutal ride, and Chandler abandoned the machine for chiropractic reasons. *Bigfoot 4x4, Inc.*

Thanks to their buoyant tires, monster trucks actually float. Bigfoot has raced a paddle-wheel boat, and Grave Digger has driven across a lake. Ms. Bigfoot negotiates a river here. *Bigfoot 4x4, Inc.*

coil-overs cost about $1,500 each, which also includes the coil springs.

Thus, coil-over shocks appeared to be the final piece in the high-tech suspension puzzle. Dennis Anderson was one of the first drivers to use the made-for-monster-trucks coil-overs from Lance King, but Bob Chandler was doing his own testing. Using nitrogen gas to pressurize the oil in the shock, Chandler had his early versions of Bigfoot 8 and 9 literally suspended on air (or, more accurately, gas). Trail Master marketed Chandler's nitro-charged design to the masses.

Currently, most monsters are dampened by Steve Combs' Knight Stalker nitrogen dampers, KS Nitro Shocks, available with as much as a 30-inch stroke. Price per nitro boinger runs about $2,000.

However, the length of the shock stroke doesn't necessarily limit a monster truck's suspension travel. Thanks to such innovators as Bob Chandler, Dan Patrick, Marty Garza, Frank Schettini, and others who've either studied architecture or raced dirt bikes, cantilevering the 4-link suspension can add a few more beyond-shock-travel inches. These swing-arm setups can give a monster

MONSTER TRUCK SPECS

Overall height: 11–12.5 feet
Overall width: 12–12.5 feet
Overall weight: 9,000–11,000 pounds
Engine: maximum 575 cubic inches
Horsepower: 1,500–2,000
Aspiration: 8–71 supercharger
Fuel: methanol or nitro-methane
Transmissions: modified 3-4-speed automatics
Axles: 5-ton military, industrial, or agricultural
Suspension: 4-link, coil-over or nitrogen-charged shocks
Tires: 66x43x25 Firestone or Goodyear terras
Wheels: 43x25 steel
Estimated top speed: 100 mph
Estimated 0–70 mph acceleration: 5 seconds
Long-jumping capability: 202 feet
Vertical leaping capability: 20-25 feet

truck about 36 inches of wheel travel. That's comparable to the highest-tech Baja Trophy Trucks (which also use swing-arm suspensions). The sickest part of all this is that suspension development is ongoing as builders continue to look for every possible edge.

Axles

Most people can partially relate to monster truck suspensions, as they've seen facsimiles in the passenger-vehicle world. Multi-link suspensions are found in everything from Jeep Grand Cherokees to Nissan economy cars, and air bags allow lowered street trucks to lay frame, get in the weeds, flick some sparks, or whatever trend has captured the day's imagination. Monster truck axles, however, have nothing in common with the vehicle in most people's garages. Instead, they rely on industrial, agricultural, and even military technology.

As tire size and weight increased, monster truck axles grew to handle the load. Early upgrades were military 2–1/2-ton axles—roughly 2–1/2 times as strong as a 1-ton pickup's pumpkins. However, aerial stunts and

Bigfoot 5 is the world's largest pickup-bodied truck. Its 10-feet-tall tires—seen here in four-wheel dually configuration—came from Alaska Pipeline supply trucks. *Bigfoot 4x4, Inc.*

The Bigfoot Shuttle was introduced in 1985 with an Econoline van body and 48-inch tires. It was later rebodied when Ford introduced the Aerostar. *Bigfoot 4x4, Inc.*

freestyle frenzies put increased responsibility on steering knuckles, gears, and other axle components.

Solutions came in a variety of forms in an attempt to find the always-elusive optimal combination of high strength and low weight: 5-ton military axles, school bus axles, tractor axles, forklift axles. Bob Chandler even combed the planet and introduced some of the German ZF (makers of many sports-car manual transmissions) industrial-duty axles to monster truckdom.

Regardless of from whence they come, monster truck axles need knuckles—these big beasts must have both front and rear steering to maneuver around tight coliseum confines. The front axle might have a somewhat-standard

belt-driven pump arrangement. Rear steering is activated by electrically driven (solenoid-actuated) hydraulic pumps, which are normally activated by a shifter-mounted button. The system is self-centering—the tires automatically return to the straight-ahead position when the button is released.

Weight is also a concern. Monster builders often shave a few pounds by scrapping the drum brakes, opting instead for discs mounted on the pinion shaft at the axles. Continuing the military heritage, many axles have gear-reduction capabilities in their hubs, similar to the original Hummer. This eases the torque load on the axle shafts.

The life of a monster mechanic can be boiled down t0 two words: changing tires. *Frank Schettini/Monster Jerky*

Field fixes—sometimes literally on the field during a race—are one of the sport's ugly realities, as the Monster Patrol team demonstrates. *Frank Schettini/Monster Jerky*

To boil down years of monster-axle lore, simply realize that—*Junkyard Wars* aside—you won't stumble across Bigfoot axles while scouring boneyards for a replacement F-350 rear end. If you do, then all bona fide gearheads will want to know where you shop.

Engines, Transmissions, and Transfer Cases

No proprietary stuff here. Most monster trucks use the good ol' American Pro Stock drag-racing setup: big-block V-8, bored and stroked to as much as 575 cubic inches, per MTRA limitations; 8-71 supercharger; nitro-methane fuel. This arrangement consistently puts out about 1,500 horsepower, although some truck builders claim to have as much as 2,000 ponies onboard.

Race-prepped automatic transmissions are the most common. Today's state-of-the-art gearbox is an air-shifted four-speed Lenco.

Most monster trucks use either a Profab or SRS transfer case to send engine power to both axles. A major advantage here is that its internal gears can be changed relatively easily (at least when compared to a light-duty 4x4's transfer case). For short tracks, when off-the-line acceleration is crucial, the transfer case will likely be geared lower (which means a higher-numbered gear ratio but greater reduction compared to engine rpm).

Tires and Wheels

Originally, the 66x43x25 tires used on monster trucks were designed for commercial fertilizer spreaders and other agricultural applications. These days, both Firestone and Goodyear make custom tires specifically for monster trucks. They cost about as much as $3,000 new. Some teams tune the treads by shaving away some of the rubber. This makes the tire a little more flexible and saves some weight. Depending on racing conditions, tire pressures often fall within the 5 to 11 psi range.

On display outside the Bigfoot 4x4 shop in Hazelwood, Missouri, Bigfoot 5 stands on 10-feet-tall tires. These were originally used on World War II land trains in Alaska. The Bigfoot trucks occasionally make exhibition appearances on these tires.

Executioner earns points in the Penda series.

One of the most disturbing-looking trucks ever, Dungeon of Doom was actually a menacing fiberglass body over the Bigfoot 8 chassis. This shot is from the 1997 Southern Jamboree Nationals.

Always pushing the envelope, Bob Chandler introduced the so-called 3-D body style with Snakebite. This fiberglass body adapted easily to the Bigfoot trucks.

Monster truck rims take a beating. Measuring 43x25 inches, they're made of steel in order to withstand the force of 10,000 pounds consistently crushing down on them. Custom one-piece models are stronger than welded-together multi-piece wheels.

Bodies

Factory-style sheet-metal bodies are a distant memory. For years now, all competitive monster trucks have worn fiberglass skin. This material is both lighter and easier to repair than metal—body damage can often be repaired by gluing a crack back together or patching in replacement pieces.

Fiberglass also allows monster owners to change bodies easier than they could with sheet metal. Some teams carry multiple bodies, swapping them as necessary to appease sponsors. The Bigfoot trucks have worn many bodies over the years. This has allowed Bob Chandler to create competition within his own camp. At any given event, one Bigfoot truck might wear the company's name while other trucks might compete in Snakebite, Firestone Wilderness, or even a WrestleTruck skin. In effect, the Bigfoot drivers go head-to-head against each other. In these situations, the fans always win. Not wanting to sustain the inevitable verbal abuse until the next race motivates the drivers to have heavier right feet than common sense might otherwise dictate.

Fiberglass bodies aren't cheap. A new mold for a wild 3-D body can cost as much as $20,000 to tool-up. After that, each body created from the mold can run $5,000. The current cost of a basic pickup-truck body rendered in fiberglass is approximately $2,500. Many teams rely on GTS Fiberglass in Wentzville, Missouri, for their bodies.

The shell, however, is just the beginning of the body story. A basic paint job over the fiberglass can average $2,000. Add in custom airbrushing and graphics along the lines of the Grave Digger murals, and the tab rapidly escalates to the $7,000 range.

Monster Maintenance

Compared to passenger cars, maintenance on a monster truck is anything but routine. Consider engine oil: Most monster truck crews change oil after a weekend of two or three runs. This is because the nitro-methane racing fuel tends to break down the oil much faster than regular gasoline does. In conjunction with the oil change, the engine's valves and lifters are often adjusted.

A general walk-around of the truck is also in order to inspect U-joints, frame welds, and fasteners. Transmissions seem to be the weak link in monster trucks, because they have to feed a tremendous amount of power to the transfer case while withstanding incredible forces from jumping and bouncing. Some crews will pull the transmission after every few shows and rebuild it *before* trouble starts.

Engines generally last about a season. Some drivers are lucky enough to get more than a year's service, while others destroy their powerplants after a few months. Most monster pilots try to find the ideal compromise between putting on an exciting show and keeping the truck mechanically fit for the next stop on the tour. Drivers usually double as monster mechanics.

Dan Patrick's Samson helped popularize the 3-D body style. Its fiberglass "guns" originally promoted the *American Gladiators* television show. This is its 1999 look.

Driving a Monster Truck

The life of a driver used to be glitzy and glamorous. As more people aspired to partake in car-crushing glory, the event promoters assumed the power. If one driver didn't want to risk destroying his truck to thrill the crowd, 20 others anxiously awaited the opportunity.

The heyday of the privateer peaked in the early 1990s. At that time, the majority of monster truck owners/drivers were contractors or technicians who held "real" jobs during the week and tried to get their trucks booked at events on weekends.

The monsters themselves are only a fraction of the overall operation. True, they're expensive to build, and costly replacement parts must be stocked in order to consistently campaign a truck. Broken monsters that disappear for months between appearances rarely develop the fan base that promoters crave. Above and beyond the monsters themselves, semi tractor-trailers have to be purchased and maintained, and over-the-road permits to operate a commercial truck in all 50 states are horribly expensive. The Grave Digger team's budget for repairs and maintenance on a monster and hauler, fuel for both, uniforms, and lodging, is more than $120,000 per year. Their cost to build a truck and stock spare parts is approximately $250,000—each Grave Digger engine reportedly runs $50,000.

The tour also takes its toll on relationships. Pam and Mike Vaters, the sport's glamorous car-crushing couple for much of the 1990s, divorced after failing to find a balance between travel and family life. Many other lower-profile relationships have suffered the same fate.

The brutal truth of the business is that most of the people who built a monster truck as a get-rich-quick scheme got the exact opposite. As a result, the sport has seen a mass exodus in recent years, particularly as technological advances make competing at a high level more expensive every year. Even popular teams have thrown in their shop rags.

On a good weekend, though, a driver does actually get paid to show off. Electricians and plumbers never

Guy Wood's Bulldozer monster proved that when you play with the bull, you sometimes get the horns.

Hulkster, inspired by wrestler Hulk Hogan, was actually a custom fiberglass body over Bigfoot 9.

experience the adrenaline rush spurred by thousands of people screaming their approval and lining up for autographs.

All males—and more females than will publicly admit to it—fantasize about driving a monster truck. The reality is, few will ever get the chance to actually do it. It used to be much easier to become a driver than it is now. The trail to monster-piloting glory followed one of two paths: You either procured your own truck or worked your way up through the ranks with an established team. In the heyday (circa late 1980s), every high-school welding-shop valedictorian apparently built his own monster truck. At *Four Wheeler*, around 1989, we even received a handwritten list (on Big Chief tablet paper, no less) from a kid who'd catalogued something

like 500 monster trucks. Hopefully that kid got some kind of school credit for his research skills. The list hung on the hallway wall for a few weeks, gaining names of trucks that just weren't meant to be: 2 TUFF 4 U 2 TOUCH, Ground-Pounding Flounder, Turbo Suppository, and other long-forgotten gems that couldn't be reprinted here, anyway. Someone ultimately sentenced the list to the circular file.

Apparently, a lot of people had easy access to military axles and 66-inch tires—or at least the phone number to Boyce Equipment, in Utah. By doing all of the welding and wrenching yourself, a bona-fide monster truck could be assembled for $70,000 or so. (Makes one wonder what those government farm subsidies are really

Did anyone ever see Hulk Hogan himself drive the monsters that cross-promoted his persona?

spent on, but that dovetails into the history of tractor pulling.) At the time, you couldn't attend a Wal-Mart grand opening in any state whose name begins with a vowel without parking near an on-display monster truck. Every monster builder had high hopes of going big-time: getting that fat auto-parts chain sponsorship, living the glamorous life on the road, and beating Bigfoot to the finish line while motorheads and babes from around the country watched on ESPN or TNN.

Many a hard-working contractor also built a monster truck to have a little fun and promote his business at the same time. A lot of these people had already participated in tractor pulling or mud racing. They knew the drill: Begin by building a vehicle on nights and weekends, or

have your employees pitch-in during normal working hours, if applicable. Once the truck is done, work the day job Monday through Thursday, get your kids, nephews, and neighbors to help load the truck onto the trailer on Thursday night, and head out to the event. Arrive at the fairgrounds on Friday, call work to verify that your employees are robbing you blind while you're away playing, and set up in the pits. Crush cars on Saturday and Sunday, have armies of kids wish that you were their real father. Take off the big tires, load up the truck, and return home. Repeat the cycle.

Sounds good? Well, racing ain't cheap. When it comes to monster trucks, a single broken part can literally put the whole operation out of business. Even Bigfoot

isn't immune. Not to drop the dime on anyone, but at a certain show years ago in a large city in the Valley of the Sun, the king of all monsters broke a shock during its Saturday afternoon maneuvers. Normally, this would be a minor inconvenience. But, hypothetically, if a crew member happened to forget to load replacement shocks onto the semi before leaving the shop, then a broken boinger could end Bigfoot's weekend prematurely. Said crew member would then be chastised by all, delaying his promotion to a Bigfoot driver's seat by months, maybe years. Even worse, kids would experience overwhelming depression when their much-beloved monster couldn't limp out of the pits on Sunday. Now consider what it's like for the teams that can't afford spare parts!

Wrestler Bill Goldberg was one of the few celebrity monster truck owners (basketball player Karl Malone another). Tom Meents won the 2001 Monster Jam title in this truck.

So, that's the average owner-operator monster truck scenario in a nutshell. Variations of this theme include the Richard Branson approach to risky businesses. When asked the best way to become a millionaire, the Virgin-branded group of companies—including Virgin Airways—mogul said something like, "Start as a billionaire, and launch your own airline." For everyone who makes a living by showing or racing a monster truck, scores of others have gone broke trying. The mutation to tube-framed monsters really weeded out aspiring monster masters—the price of admission now included designing/engineering and then fabricating a truck from scratch that bore absolutely no resemblance to a stock vehicle.

Hitch a Ride

Car-compacting is counter-intuitive. For one, human instinct aims our eyes forward. When the monster goes airborne over a line of junked cars, only a thin band of sky fills the forward field of vision between the hood's front edge and the overhead roofline. Instead, proper driving technique is to watch the ground through the clear-plastic firewall and floorboard. This allows the driver to watch the front tires' position, something that isn't always apparent while airborne.

The most common first-time driver mistake happens in mid-air. Instinct apparently makes the right foot lift off the accelerator. The front tires stop spinning, and the monster truck falls from the sky like a 10,000-pound asteroid—attempting to auger itself into the

Rear steering is actuated by this button on the shift knob.

This office is all business. Thick Lexan plastic allows the driver to see the tires and ground through the floorboard and wheel wells, as *Popular Mechanics* writer Ben Stewart learned.

ground. According to *Popular Mechanics* writer Ben Stewart, the key to car-crushing success is "keeping the meats in motion," blipping the throttle while airborne to keep the tires spinning. This helps transfer the impact from purely downward force to somewhat forward momentum upon reentry to the Earth's surface. Otherwise, the driver's body absorbs abuse that's comparable to being strapped onto an office chair and thrown out a second-story window. (Another way to saddle up a monster is to get your own national late-night talk show and invite Bigfoot to participate in a segment.)

Those in the know claim that the adrenaline rush spurred by piloting a 1,500-horsepower, 5-ton machine masks the spinal pain. The closest the rest of us will come is at the joystick of a video game.

Big, Dumb Jerkiness: Fringe Innovations

Frank Schettini was a southern California kid with a dream to be a pro beach volleyball player. When he quit

growing (significantly short of the stature required to be King of the Beach), Frank modified his dream.

A metal-shop junkie in high school, Frank was driving the tallest truck in town shortly after getting his driver's license. When Frank saw his first monster truck race, in the 1980s, he refocused his life to a single goal: beating Bigfoot. Living in Los Angeles, Frank was thousands of miles away from the hotbeds of monster trucks, both geographically and culturally. Most drivers and crew members from the Golden Era of Monster Trucks (mid-1980s to mid-1990s) wore the mandatory mullet hair style. Frank had a flat-top with front swoop, kind of like lead singers in bad British new-wave bands at the time.

Frank had an ace up his sleeve, though. Like many southern Californians, he rode dirt bikes, and Frank started racing motocross at age 18. He began fabricating his own motorcycle parts in an attempt to gain a competitive edge. Frank also customized his trucks. While

Truck groupies: The monsters are the stars of the show. Much to the driver's chagrin, the Big Dummy Cheerleaders (circa 1989) only cared about the truck. *Frank Schettini/Monster Jerky*

Big Dummy 3 was a prime example of an exhibition monster. With a body that raised hydraulically on a scissors-lift subframe and a tilt-bed full of stereo speakers, it always attracted a crowd. *Frank Schettini/Monster Jerky*

attending college, his daily-driven truck on 40-inch tires attracted attention. The Chevy became known as Big Dummy after an unimpressed coed described it as "big and dumb." But at shows throughout the Southwest, custom-truck fans admired Frank's work. Overloaded with requests from people wanting Frank to work on their trucks, he opened Unlimited Customs, a shop specializing in 4x4 suspensions.

In 1990, Frank decided to transform his daily driver into a monster truck to promote Unlimited Customs. Known as Big Dummy 3, the Chevy's body was mounted to a scissors-lift subframe that could raise the truck's ride height to about 10 feet. Suicide doors, a tilt bed, and a competition sound system were a few of its other features. Bid Dummy 3 appeared at car and truck shows, sporting events, birthday parties, and grand openings throughout California, Arizona, and Nevada. Magazine exposure led to television commercials and even motion-picture parts for Frank and his truck.

Still a racer at heart, Frank decided that he needed to build a competition monster. Frank compared notes with Bob Chandler and Dan Patrick, then he relied on his own motocross experience to design Big Dummy IV. Noticing that monster trucks lost a lot of time in the turns and often suffered carburetor problems while airborne, Frank schemed up innovative solutions to these shortcomings.

Re-engineering: Frank Schettini wasn't happy with his first attempt at Big Dummy 4 (now Monster Jerky). He solved geometry problems by borrowing suspension angles from his Yamaha YZ450 dirt bike. *Frank Schettini/Monster Jerky*

Monster Jerky is controlled by handlebars and pedals. The advantages are greater control in corners and less impact on the driver's body. *Frank Schettini/Monster Jerky*

His overall concept was to create an enormous four-wheeled dirt bike. Handlebars and foot pedals would control the throttle and allow independent braking of each side to better control slides and set up turns. By suspending himself in a harness and standing on foot pegs, Frank also minimizes driver damage: His knees absorb the brunt of the impacts, not his back. When designing the frame, Frank cribbed fork- and swing-arm angles from his YZ450 dirt bike. He burned dumpsters full of welding rod and steel tubing before arriving at the final design.

Big Dummy 4 was originally designed to compete in the Special Events Penda Points series. Noticing that the typical monster's Predator carburetors didn't always feed fuel consistently when off-the-level, Frank pursued an alternative-fuel solution. Propane proved promising. This fuel turns from liquid to gas as it leaves its storage tank. So, unlike liquid fuel sloshing around in a carburetor, vehicle angle doesn't affect gaseous propane's fuel delivery. Propane also burns clean. Its lack of toxic byproducts makes propane well-suited to indoor shows.

Naked monster: Extensive triangulation is visible in Frank Schettini's Monster Jerky. For competition, he stands on foot pegs and is suspended in a harness. *Frank Schettini/Monster Jerky*

Cantilevered swing-arms (in blue) allow suspension travel to exceed the stroke length of the shock absorber. *Frank Schettini/Monster Jerky*

Then Frank gave his Chevy big-block engine some extra boost. To force in as much air as possible, Frank added a turbocharger—to each cylinder. The engine looked like Frank had hit a hair dryer close-out sale on QVC. But just as Frank finished his truck, the Penda Series went away, and rule changes caused him to return to a more traditional engine setup. He currently competes at shows in the western states, preferring to do business with local, independent promoters.

Handlebar-controlled Monster Jerky (nee Big Dummy 4) is basically just an overgrown dirt bike with two extra tires and a blown V-8 engine. *Frank Schettini/Monster Jerky*

CHAPTER 5

ADULTHOOD
ALL GROWN UP

To many Americans, monster trucks remain a Jeff Foxworthy punchline. The fact that almost everyone who drove a monster truck during the sport's golden era, the mid-1980s to mid-1990s, sported a mullet (Pam Vaters Vahe included) perpetuated the industry's white-trash elan.

Hardcore fans and astute motorheads know otherwise. A single monster truck can create more excitement than 12 hockey players on the exact same piece of space. Even the occasional NASCAR driver who does a test run in a monster dismounts the machine in utter awe. While most competitive drivers understand the physics of forward momentum and side forces, only monster truck drivers and desert racers know the importance of sticking a landing with four wheels under control. Monster trucks throw 10,000 pounds into the equation, which makes the dynamics even more interesting.

To state the obvious another way, racing is a serious motorsport. As Dennis Anderson said after ramming Grave Digger into a wall and breaking a knee in 1991, "It's a real serious motorsport. A lot of people think we're some kind of damn circus act." And the monster truck industry is at its best during side-by-side competition—ideally outdoors in a large enough venue to include turns. But first, we must digress.

Commercialization

As the Hollywood cliché goes, "It's called show *business* for a reason: Without the business, there is no show." Because monster trucks arguably appeal to the human imagination more than any other form of motorized entertainment, marketing schemes for them are always brewing.

Exhibit A is what's now known as WrestleTrucks. The freak-show overtones of the average show parallel that of professional wrestling. Their respective audiences obviously also overlap. So it didn't take a genius talent agent to team up the Bigfoot and World Championship Wrestling (WCW) in 1995. The facts that monster trucks were beginning to sport 3-D fiberglass bodies and their drivers exuded unassuming personalities made the industry ripe for some in-your-face, trash-talking cross promotion. Monster trucks literally became promotional vehicles for Hulk Hogan, Sting, The Undertaker, and other wrestlers. True monster fans mourned the industry's loss of its own identity and purpose during this era: "Good" trucks and "heel" monsters were tough for many to digest. Ford, Chevy, and Mopar were the only rivalries the fans needed. Incidentally, wrestler Bill Goldberg was one of the few insiders to apparently take the alliance seriously. Instead of letting someone else license his name, Goldberg actually partnered with former Monster Patrol

Side-by-side racing graduated monster trucks from a novelty to a bona fide motorsport. Few drive harder year after year than Grave Digger's Dennis Anderson.

Mark and Tim Hall stormed the 2002 season with the Rammunition and Raminator Dodges.

driver Tom Meents to campaign a truck. They won the 2001 Monster Jam Championship.

Promoters

Entertainers and promoters traditionally have an adversarial relationship. They need each other, but promoters control the cash flow. The promoter collects the gate, and (like musical acts) the owner relies on said promoter to share the wealth. Contracts are good on paper, but when there aren't many games in town, the little guy often hesitates to rock the boat and risk getting blackballed.

Politics are the ugly underbelly of every industry, monster trucks included. Promoters have shaped the recent history of monster trucks—and not always with the sport's best interest in mind—and will undoubtedly steer their future.

Once, there were many promoters. Now, there are two big ones. Just a few of the names that have been attached to monster truck shows since the 1980s are Pace, Special Events, SFX, SRO, TNT, USA Motorsports, and USHRA. Special Events remains, and the other names have merged and acquisitioned into Clear Channel Entertainment (CCE), a conglomerate that produces live entertainment in addition to owning radio and television stations, as well as billboards. In 2000, Pace (now CCE) eliminated the distinction between promoter and performer: It bought several monster truck teams, Grave Digger being the highest-profile.

Business-wise, having the performers on the payroll makes sense. Trucks and drivers can be assigned to various shows, eliminating the "scheduled to appear" independent contractor component of event promotion. The drawback is that competitors who don't work for the promoter feel that the deck is stacked against them. After all, if a promoter already has his own trucks and drivers on his spreadsheet, how anxious is he to have to pay prize money to someone other than himself? The fact that a promoter's employee controls the ignition "kill" switch tends to make non-company drivers even more nervous. Another concern is that the promoter wants to own all video rights for potential television and

The Iceman falleth from the sky: Steve Macklyn purchased the Executioner Chevy from the Hall Brothers and reinvented it as something more appropriate to his Salt Lake City hometown.

home-video use, preventing individual teams from producing their own commercial videos at CCE events.

ProMT

CCE's perceived attempt to monopolize monster truck shows led Bob Chandler to launch ProMT (Professional Monster Trucks), with legendary Bigfoot driver Eric Meagher serving as president. Purely a sanctioning organization, ProMT's method of operation is to ally with a promoter to produce a points series. All trucks must comply with MTRA safety and minimum-weight standards—9,500 pounds—to participate in ProMT. Lighter trucks (CCE minimum is 9,000 pounds) were required to add weights to bulk up. Also, the organization's original charter was racing-based: no 3-D bodies or freestyle exhibitions. The ProMT competition format

Generation X delights the crowd at the 2000 Spring Jamboree.

calls for open qualifying and a 12-truck roster for each event. However, provisional spots were granted to top-10 finishers from the previous year's series.

Rules were modified after ProMT's inaugural season. By fan request, 3-D bodies were allowed, but they were limited to designs that retained some resemblance to a factory truck. An acceptable example is Samson: Its 3-D arms don't obscure its identifiable Chevy Silverado styling cues. In 2002, ProMT also relaxed its ban on freestyle, again to appease the fans. Following the racing, four to six trucks were allowed to strut their stuff as time allowed. It was purely an exhibition, not a judged competition.

ProMT ran three successful seasons (2000–2002) at NASCAR speedways, with Truxpo as the event promoter.

Special Events

The "outdoor series," Special Events has included monster trucks in its Jamboree Nationals truck shows since 1983. In contrast to CCE's primarily indoor and stadium shows, Special Events usually books fairground facilities. This allows the track designers more space to get creative. Since many Special Events shows also include mud racing and a tough-truck competition, the monsters have plenty of raw material for freestyle antics. In fact, many of Bigfoot's "firsts" were actually impromptu stunts

Krimson Krusher taking a Sunday drive at the 2000 Fall Jamboree Nationals.

at Special Events Jamboree shows. At any given show, fans might see Bigfoot clear (and clear out) the mud pit. Also, the distance-jumping craze was hatched at a Fall Jamboree Nationals in Indianapolis after Bigfoot driver Jim Kramer hit the line of junk cars especially fast and cleared 'em without crushing 'em. For Sunday's finale, Kramer got a substantial run from the far end of the fairgrounds and cleared 13 side-by-side junkers.

Overall, Special Events has been a boon to the sport over the years. Its Penda Points Series was a fan and driver favorite in the 1990s, and many a monster truck started as a Show-N-Shine contestant at a Jamboree Nationals show. Throughout, Special Events has remained relatively apolitical. Bigfoot trucks have been show mainstays over the years, and Special Events has invited Grave Digger and other CCE-owned trucks to participate recently.

Monster Truck Madness

There are numerous trends that have appeared and, in some cases, disappeared through the years. In order to captivate interest and investigate potential areas of popularity among fans, drivers, and promoters alike, monster trucking has branched out from the events one saw during earlier eras of the sport.

Freestyle: The Art of Monster Expressionism

Freestyle represents a return to the roots of monster trucks. These beasts began as an exhibition spectacle before that inherent American desire to compete shifted the format of the average monster show.

Apparently, though, regular racing didn't allow drivers to fully express themselves. Some began doing burn-outs and donuts, either to get the crowd worked up for a race or to celebrate a victory. Then, egos and one-upmanship entered the picture. By the mid-1990s, many drivers were doing exhibition routines, somewhat the equivalent of the floor exercise in Olympic gymnastics. These goof-off sessions got progressively longer until more time was being spent freestyling than actually racing.

Racing purists hated any aspect of the sport that wasn't tied to a stopwatch. But the average fan went wild for the freestyle. The pure athleticism exhibited by these 10,000-pound machines actually brought newfound respect to monster trucks. The fact that a lot of crashes occurred when drivers got caught up in the excitement and couldn't pull their feet off the accelerators made for great event coverage. Many of the outrageous photos in this book were shot during the freestyle portions of monster shows.

Astute promoters realized that freestyle was a fan favorite. Freestyle programs became official components of many shows starting around 1996. Other promoters looked at freestyle as an aberration that detracted from

Freestyle gives monster drivers the chance to totally trash their equipment. Kirk Dabney is usually up to the task. Here, Extreme Overkill wasn't.

the racing. In fact, the original ProMT game plan strictly forbade freestyle.

For the time being, freestyle looks like it's here to stay. Crowd response is overwhelmingly positive—people like carnage, and freestyle gives drivers carte blanche to destroy their trucks. It's also created an elite class of monster maniacs who fearlessly push their trucks to the limit—and sometimes beyond—at every show. Stand-out freestylers include Dennis Anderson, Kirk Dabney, Dan Runte, and Mike Vaters.

Sideshows: Tanks And Transformers

The P. T. Barnum coefficient of early monster truck shows led critics to dismiss these beasts as an unfortunate trend. Monster trucks were lumped in the same dumpster as the pet rock and new wave synth-pop music.

Part of the credibility problem was that monsters started as a motorsports sideshow. As soon as they became headliners, monsters promptly got their own sideshow. Any large mutant machine was apparently welcome to perform at a monster truck show.

These beasts arose from within. Always looking for the next big thing (literally), Bob Chandler was one of the first to build a monster tank. Known as Bigfoot Fastrax, it originally appeared as a Ford E350 van body mounted on a tracked M84 military personnel carrier. Weighing more than 23,000 pounds, Fastrax was powered by two Ford 460 big-block V-8s. The vehicle was later rebodied with 1990 Ford Aerostar sheet metal.

Other prominent monster tanks included the Virginia Giant and Equalizer. Although a novelty for the fans, these car-crushing tanks weren't driver-friendly.

Monster trucks inspired outrageous creativity. Robosaurus thrilled crowds at monster truck shows by literally eating junked cars. *Frank Schettini/Monster Jerky*

They lacked suspension, so their drivers' bodies jolted and flailed as the tanks drove over junked cars.

Even more outrageous than monster tanks were the so-called transformers. Apparently inspired by kids' toys, these machines would unfold themselves into fire-breathing, car-eating monstrosities. Their sheer ridiculousness delighted kids and was a guilty pleasure for many adults—although few would admit that (at least with a straight face). Robosaurus, Megasarus, and Vorian are three of this species' best-known examples.

Pro Stock Class: Mini-Monster Racing

Privateers have basically been priced out of the monster market. The cost of building a truck and feeding a team is so high these days that most monsters are owned by multi-truck conglomerates. The one-truck owner/operator era is now a memory.

As monster trucks become more high-tech and expensive, they're harder to relate to. Just as Winston Cup cars only vaguely resemble the offerings at a dealer's showroom, monster trucks have lost a lot of their realistic and personal appeal.

In 1997, Sam and Jill Marino hatched a plan to restore some average-fan appeal to monster trucks. Their proposed Pro Stock class called for a maximum tire size of 48 inches. The main benefit is that a Pro Stock truck could be built for a fraction of the cost, $15,000–$20,000, in the Marinos' estimation. This cost includes nitrogen

Sam Marino tried to launch a 48-inch-tire Pro Stock Class in the mid-1990s. His goal: restoring affordability to monster truck racing.

John Hartsock launches Sudden Impact with authority.

Dave Richard's Maine-iac was one of the few remaining leaf-sprung trucks in the mid-1900s.

shocks, a full roll cage, and even a competitive motor. Best of all, Pro Stock would allow the non-millionaire enthusiast an opportunity to build a truck and compete. Participant growth would fuel the sport as a result. Also, teams that were struggling financially in the 66-inch world could step down and conceivably continue to campaign a truck.

Sam did numerous exhibitions in his Raptor Dodge on the East Coast in the late 1990s to prove that these mini-monsters could fly as high, turn tighter, and generally generate as much excitement as the big boys. Sam even lobbied the MTRA to create the new class, hoping that existing teams would jump on the Pro Stock bandwagon.

Holman's Beast has more air under its tires than is in them.

Unfortunately, the bigger-is-better mentality prevailed. Some existing drivers and promoters weren't convinced that fans would embrace these not-quite bigger-than-life trucks. Maybe Sam and Jill Marino simply had a great idea that was ahead of its time.

The Finish Line

So, where is the monster truck industry today? They're undoubtedly still a force to be reckoned with. Not that anyone associated with them gives a damn anymore

Bigfoot paint schemes seem to change with the seasons—and sponsors. Flames were in fashion for this event.

Maybe four-wheel drive is overrated. This driver gets the job done with one-wheel drive.

about mainstream credibility, but CCE recently made a giant gesture aimed at appeasing the public at large: The promoter sponsored an extensive, interactive exhibit titled Monster Trucks: The Science of Extreme Machines, at the Museum of Science and Industry in Chicago.

Monster trucks have also had a profound influence on contemporary culture. The combination of human imagination, creation, and machinery first demonstrated by Bob Chandler in 1974 manifests itself nearly nightly on cable television. Without monster trucks, we

Big Dawg gets off the porch.

Perfect 10s: Mike Vaters gets his 10,000-pound Black Stallion at least 10 feet in the air over Andy Hoffman's Nitemare at the 1999 Summer Jamboree.

Ever wonder what happened to the custom-van craze? Monster trucks seem to have dealt it a final death blow.

might not have *Junkyard Wars, Battle Bots,* and *Monster Garage*–all mandatory viewing for innovative-machine aficionados. And try as the rest of the world might, non-North Americans have failed to build proper high-flying monster trucks.

Monsters of the future will be even lighter and more powerful. As a result, they'll accelerate and stop faster, fly higher and farther. Monster trucks will continue to entertain billions of people worldwide. Laugh at them if you like, but those in the know laugh *with* them. Their underlying technology and uninhibited performance make monster trucks anything but a joke.

Guy Wood needs a Hawaiian vacation after this Tropical Thunder landing.

APPENDIX 1

MONSTER TRUCK TIMELINE

1925   Henry Ford introduces the Model T Runabout, the first mass-produced pickup truck.

1972   Bob Chandler fits oversized tires on his 1967 Ford 4x4 pickup.

1974   Bob and Marilyn Chandler open Midwest Four Wheel Drive Center in Hazelwood, Missouri. They purchase a 1974 Ford F-250 as a shop truck.

Bob Chandler's F-250 goes through 18 tire and wheel combinations before settling on 1200–16.5 (about 32-inches tall) farm-implement tires.

1976   Bob Chandler's Truck is christened "Bigfoot."

1977   Bob Chandler "crashes" the Specialty Equipment Market Association (SEMA) automotive parts and accessories trade show in Las Vegas. Bigfoot steals the show.

1978   Bigfoot gets rear steering, making it a 4x4x4.

1979   Bigfoot's first paid appearance is at a Denver car show.

1980   SRO promoter Bob George coins the phrase "monster truck."

1981   Bob Chandler performs the first-ever car crush in Bigfoot, which now rides on 48-inch tires, in a field near his shop. A videotape of the event becomes an underground favorite.

Bigfoot makes a cameo in *Take This Job and Shove It,* making it the first monster truck to appear in a feature movie.

Dennis Anderson builds a 1951 Ford panel-van-bodied mud racer in a Virginia chicken coop.

1982   Bigfoot 2 built.

1983   The first monster truck on 66-inch tires, Bigfoot 2, crushes cars during a truck pull and nearly incites a riot at the Pontiac Silverdome, in Detroit.

1984   The first exclusively monster truck show is held at Pontiac Silverdome.

Built in fall 1983, Bigfoot 3 debuts in January 1984 at the Pontiac Silverdome on dual 66-inch tires at each corner.

Bigfoot 4 built.

Battle of the Monster Trucks debuts.

1985   Bigfoot Ranger mini-truck bodied monster and Bigfoot Shuttle van-bodied vehicle built.

Marilyn Chandler becomes the first woman to drive a monster truck.

1986   Bigfoot 5 unveiled on 10-feet-tall tires.

Bigfoot 6 built.

First-ever monster race held at the Houston Astrodome.

Bigfoot conquers the colossal 170-feet-tall Big Elim hill at Gravelrama in Cleves, Ohio.

1987   Sanctioned by the U.S. Hot Rod Association (USHRA), side-by-side monster truck racing begins.

Monster Truck Racing Association (MTRA) formed.

Jim Kramer (Bigfoot 6) jumps 13 cars, claiming the first world-distance record.

1988   Everett Jasmer (USA-1) wins Renegades TNT Monster Truck Challenge, the first points series.

Bigfoot 7 built.

Bigfoot Fastrax tank unveiled.

Dennis Anderson and Grave Digger join the circuit.

TNT-produced *Tuff Trax* television series airs on ESPN, TNN, and in syndication.

1989 Jack Willman (Taurus) builds the first four-link coil-over race truck.

Bob Chandler creates Bigfoot 8, the first tube-chassis truck designed completely on Auto CAD.

1990 Bear Foot wins USHRA/Camel Mud & Monsters series.

Andy Brass and Bigfoot 8 win TNT Monster Truck Challenge Series.

1991 Carolina Crusher wins the first Special Events Penda Points Series.

Taurus wins USHRA/Camel Mud & Monsters Series. The series airs on TNN as *Trucks & Tractor Power*.

Snakebite appears as the first 3-D bodied truck.

1992 Andy Brass and Bigfoot 10 win Special Events Penda Points Series monster truck championships.

First Blood wins USHRA title.

Bear Foot wins Camel Mud & Monsters Series.

1993 325 monster trucks unofficially in existence.

Bigfoot 11, rebodied as Wildfoot, wins Special Events Penda Points Series championship.

Bear Foot wins USHRA/Camel Mud & Monsters series.

Dan Patrick popularizes 3-D fiberglass bodies by adding arms to the front fenders of Samson to promote the *American Gladiators* television show.

1995 Bigfoot and monster trucks combine with WCW. WrestleTrucks result.

Halloween Havoc pay-per-view event pits monster trucks in sumo-wrestling format.

Pam Vaters (Boogey Van) becomes first MTRA-certified woman driver.

1996 Fred Shafer (Bear Foot) sets world record jump of 141 feet, 1 inch.

1997 Dan Patrick patents 3-D body design as seen on Samson.

Eric Meagher (Snakebite) wins Special Events Monster Truck Point Series.

Sam and Jill Marino (Raptor) try to start Pro Stock class for 48-inch-tired monster trucks.

Monster trucks reportedly generate more revenue than U.S. ski industry.

Promotion company Pace debuts *Inside Monster Jam,* hosted by Jerry Bernardo, on ESPN2.

1998 Dan Runte (Bigfoot) sets world-record jump of 141 feet, 10 inches.

Bigfoot debuts Firestone Wilderness Bigfoot, the first monster truck with full corporate sponsorship.

1999 Promoter Pace/SFX begins buying monster truck teams, most notably Dennis Anderson's Grave Digger operation.

Pace follows in Bigfoot's steps and enters promotional relationship with WCW.

TNN's *Motor Madness* melds monster trucks with wrestling, and Motorsports fans resent the cheesy attempts at plots.

Dan Runte jumps a Boeing 747 in Bigfoot 14, sets distance record at 202 feet.

2000 The Truxpo/ProMT Series revives points racing at major speedways around the country. Eric Tack and Firestone Wilderness win the inaugural championship.

Clear Channel Entertainment purchases Pace/SFX and becomes the largest promoter of shows and owner of the most trucks.

2001 Tom Meents and Goldberg win Monster Jam World Championships.

Monster tank revival includes Battle Kat (Mike Vaters) and Heavy Metal (Hall Brothers).

Dan Runte and Bigfoot win ProMT series.

2002 Mark Hall and Raminator win ProMT series.

Truxpo folds.

APPENDIX 2

Contacts and Resources

Monster Truck Web Sites

Aftershock, www.aftershockmtracing.com
Airborne Ranger, www.rangermotorsports.com
American Dream, www.turpenmotorsports.com
American Guardian, www.americanguardian4x4.com
Arachnophobia, www.team-kcm.com
Avenger, www.avengerracing.com
Backdraft, www.backdraftmonstertruck.com
Bad Influence, www.xtremeracin.com
Bad News, www.bds4x4.com
Bad News Travels Fast, www.badnewsracing.com
Bear Foot, www.shafermotorsports.com
Big Dawg, www.bigdawg4x4.com
Big Swede, www.bigswede.com
Bigfoot 4x4, www.bigfoot4x4.com
Bigfoot Europe (Bigfoot 17), www.bigfoot4x4.co.uk
BlackJack, www.marylandmonsters.com
Black Stallion, www.blackstallion4x4.com
Black Widow, www.pwrhouse.com/blackwidow
Blown Thunder, www.blownthunder.com
Boogey Van, www.shafer-motorsports.com
Boston BigShot, www.twrex4x4.homestead.com
Bounty Hunter, bountyhunter4x4.com
The Broker, www.thebrokernt.com
Brothers of Destruction,
     www.wwfmonstertrucks.com
Buffalo Hunter, www.wwfmonstertrucks.com
Cardiac Arrest, www.geocities.com/raaboffrd
Carolina Crusher, www.shafer-motorsports.com
Cyclone, www.phantommotorsports.org
Destroyer, www.destroyermonstertruck.com
Devil's Dodge, www.devilsdodge.com
Dragon Slayer, www.team-kcm.com
The Enforcer, www.teampossibilities.com
Equalizer, www.equalizerracing.com
Eradicator, www.suddenimpact.com
Extreme Overkill, truckworld.com/overkill
Extreme Team, www.extremeteamride.com
Firemouth,
     www.mdrags.homestead.com/truckbrandon.html

Fly-N-Hi, www.fly-n-hi.com/monster.htm
Frankenstein, www.shafer-motorsports.com
Full Boar, www.fullboarracing.com
Gator, www.bds4x4.com
GForce, www.goliath4x4.com
Godzilla,
     www.amsoil.com/monstertruck/godzilla.htm
Goliath, www.goliath4x4.com
Grave Digger, www.gravedigger.com
Ground Pounder, www.groundpounder.com
Gun Slinger, www.gunslinger4x4.com
Hercules, www.silverstone.fortunecity.com/healey/515
High Intent, www.bds4x4.com
High Voltage, www.monster-truck.com
Holman's Beast, www.teambeast.com
Hot Stuff, www.monster-truck.com
Jurassic Attack, www.jurassicattack.com
Kane, www.wwfmonstertrucks.com
Kaptain Insane, www.team-kcm.com
Keystone Krusher, www.members.accessus.net/~omiotek
King Krunch, www.kingkrunch.com
Knight Stalker, www.knight-stalker-ent.com
Krocadile Hunta, www.wwfmonstertrucks.com
Lon-Ranger, www.xtremeracin.com
Lone Wolf, www.phantommotorsports.org
Madusa, www.madusa.com
Maniac, www.jurassicattack.com
Maximum Torc, www.teambeast.com
Megasaurus, www.megasaurus.com
Mercenary, www.bds4x4.com
Michigan Rookie, www.rookie.monsterhighway.net
Misbehavin', www.team-kcm.com
Mischievous, www.team-kcm.com
Monster Jerky, www.monsterjerky.com
Monster Patrol, www.shafer-motorsports.com
The Mummy, www.shafer-motorsports.com
Nasty Boy, www:SMTR.8m.com/
Nitecrawler Tank, www.nitemare4x4.com
Nitemare, www.nitemare4x4.com
Obsession, www.obsessionracing.com

Ozz Monster, www.shafer-motorsports.com
Phantom, www.phantommotorsports.org
Pony Express, www.turpenmotorsports.com
Predator, www.predatorracinginc.com
Prowler, www.predatorracinginc.com
Pure Adrenaline, www.pureadrenalin4x4.com
Quadzilla, www.Quadzilla4X4.com
Ragin Steel, www.gunslinger4x4.com
Raminator, www.raminator.com
Rammunition, www.raminator.com
Reptoid, www.reptoid.com
The Rock, www.wwfmonstertrucks.com
Rolling Thunder, www.rollingthunder4x4x4.com
Ruff Time, www.rufftime.net
Samson, www.samson4x4.com
Scarlet Bandit, www.bountyhunter4x4.com
Shocker, www.4shocker.com
Shockwave, www.shockwave4x4.com
Skeletor, www.skeletor4x4.com
Snakebite, www.bigfoot4x4.com
Stone Cold, www.wwfmonstertrucks.com
Sudden Impact, www.suddenimpact.com
Taurus, www.shafer-motorsports.com
Tazmanian Devil, www.users.vianet.ca/~mantaz
Temporarily Insane, www.twrex4x4.homestead.com
The Terminator www.teampossibilities.com
Thrasher, www.thrasher4x4.com
Thunderfoot, www.thunderfoot.co.uk
Thunder Beast, www.monstermania.com/tbeast
Thunder Struck, www.team-kcm.com
Tornado, www.tornadotruck.tripod.com
Towasaurus Wrex, www.twrex4x4.homestead.com
Transaurus, www.transaurus.com
Tremor, www.phantommotorsports.org
Twisted Attitude, www.twistedconcepts.com
The Undertaker, www.wwfmonstertrucks.com
Unnamed and Untamed,
   www.smtr.8m.com
Virginia Giant, www.virginiagiant.com
War Wagon, www.wildfiremfg.com
Wild Child, www.shafer-motorsports.com
Wild Child,
   www.supertrux.com/WildChildMonsterTruck.htm

Wildfire, www.wwfmonstertrucks.com
Wild Hair, www.wildhair4x4.com
Wild Thang, www.shafer-motorsports.com
Willy Badd, www.perrinmotorsports.com
Xtreme Warrioir, www.phntommotorsports.org
Xtreme Whiplash, www.whiplash.monsterhighway.net

Safety Organizations
Monster Truck Racing Association (MTRA),
   www.truckworld.com/mtra
Monster Truck Racing Association Europe (MTRAE),
   www.mtrae.co.uk

Promoters
Checkered Flag Productions, www.cfpracing.com
Clear Channel Entertainment/U.S. Hot Rod
   Association (*Inside Monster Jam*), www.ushra.com
Image Promotions/Monster Nationals,
   www.monsternationals.com
J&K Motorsports, www.norcalmonsters.com
Milestone Motorsports,
   www.milestonemotorsports.com
Live Promotions, www.truckfest.co.uk
Performance Promotions, www.monstertrucks.ca
Special Events/The Promotion Company,
   www.familyevents.com

Webzines/Bulletin Boards

Monster Mania, www.monstermania.com
Monster Mayhem, http://monstermayhem.cjb.net
Monster Truck Central,
   www.MonsterTruckCentral.Homestead.com
MonsterTrucks.Net, www.monstertrucks.net
Monster Trucks UK, www.monstertrucks-uk.com
Monster Style, www.monster-style.com
Monster World,
   www.angelfire.com/wi/monsterworld
TruckWorld Online!, www.truckworld.com

Classifieds
Monster Highway's Trading Center,
   www.mttradingcenter.com

INDEX

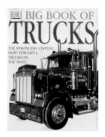
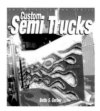
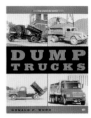
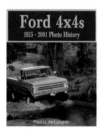

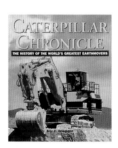
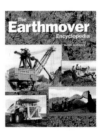